The Ever Present

Collapse

Scott Laudati

Dedication: For Andrew Joseph Stack and Mick "Mankind" Foley - the People's Champions. And Erik Perrella, for the name.

Contents

Wait For It

There's not a high enough hill on earth to stand on and scream for God. I can see you. Above the trees. A long blue sky with big fleece clouds. Pointing your finger straight up. Demanding first salvation, then a few dollars, and finally, just acknowledgment. But He never shows. How can that surprise you? You were never able to get us on the ground to stop laughing at you. You think God is going to turn the television down?

Hollywood Rain

You started off looking for Rome like I did.
In poems, in love letters,
written for a city planes fly to every day
but you knew
or decided
you hadn't earned it yet.
So
you went to West Hollywood,
a walk each night down Sunset,
not exactly The Malecón
or The Rue des Rosiers
but the girls are skinny
and sometimes you follow the one
with the German Shepard
up Rodeo
to a house her father couldn't afford
until they painted the walls
with Sharon and her baby.
The neighbors thought a murder
would sink the value but they forgot
the California sun can
baptize anything.
And when the tourists come
she puts her yoga mat in front of the bay window,
falling into downward dog
like she doesn't know what she's doing.
And the men snap pictures of her
stretched out on this cursed land,
almost as rare
as a Hollywood rain
but nowhere near as beautiful.

This Time, It Was Going To Be Me

Tonight
I decided it
was time to be
the other guy.

Some men
cannot
figure out women.
I too
was one of those men.
And
in earlier times
I would take the same
strategy of defeat.
"Nice guys finish last,"
I'd say.
"Someday they'll all want me
and they won't have me."

But someday never
came
and
the bars kept closing
and the girls
never went
home
alone.
So, when a Slovakian girl
with eyes

like a blue Hawaiian
lost
on a subway in the
cool part
of New York
looked at me and
said,
"I want the american
experience", I knew
it was time to change
tactics.

We bought a flask bottle
and went to
St. Mark's.
Even if
she
didn't dig the freak show
I knew we could find weed.
Bob Dylan
lived here, I said.
  Cool.
Bukowski
wrote right here, I said,
on this stoop.
  Cool.
I pointed at
the St. Mark's Hotel,
and that's where
Sid
killed
Nancy.
I knew something

about my facts was
wrong, but I didn't
stop.
She held the flask up
to her mouth.
I took it and
kissed her
before she could
say
cool.

Later,
we said
goodnight
and I moved
down
7th avenue.
I looked up
and
saw the Hotel Chelsea.
EVERYTHING
I had told that curious
Slovakian had been a lie.
Bob, Bukowski, dog diced Nancy,
they had all lived here,
not St. Mark's.
And then
I smiled
because
she'd
never know the
difference and
I

got to kiss her
anyway.

Tonight
I decided it
was time to be
the other guy,
and
I won.

What Are You Good At?

I don't remember when it started
but the end came last Tuesday.
I'd taken a Xanax and slept all day,
seeing an old girlfriend
and my dead dog
in dreams or nightmares
or some other hell that I'll get relive
if I don't get this one right.
And when I finally woke
I couldn't ignore what all the bad poems
and awful music had been telling me:
I'd lived too long,
there aren't going to be new chapters in my book,
there won't be any more songs.
This can happen to some at ninety
and others at thirty.
But I think for most it never happens
and that's why rationale people still breed
without any fear
of consequence.
Don't they see the holes in everything?
Don't they know there's no second coming?
Most people start dying from the minute
they're born. It
took me thirty-five years to give up
and sometimes
I'm still proud of that.
The world didn't want a new poet,
but there's always room for another plumber.

Lucky Us

I knew love once.
It was back before
my first execution.
Before the hounds were released
and the hunt was easy for fresh blood.
Back when I sat on my floor and
pictured a wild west
and if my mom asked me what I was doing
I'd say, "Listening to music."
And she'd smile at the simple world
that once spun so slow
an old record could
take up whole nights.

But not now.

Not since I opened and closed
and forgot to buy postcards in
Havana and Minneapolis.
And if I promised to let people know
I was still alive
I didn't remember or worry
because somewhere along the way
I learned
no one really cares.
And the girls don't need
a prince on a horse
by the time they're ready to kiss
their fathers goodbye.

They just want what's there.
And if it hasn't gotten drunk and
beaten them yet
it's worth saving.

Inventing a history is easier than thinking about
what might have been.
Who needs love anyway?
A new show premieres every night at eight.

Something Like Love

I miss you,
blue eyes.
Lying in your
bed
while you walked
across campus.
Looking at
Jersey mountains
rolling away from your path
like the sleeping stomachs
of giant buddhas
and me staying
warm,
making the bed
so we could unmake it.
Using your roommate's
teapot to bring
your small bones back to
life.
And your soft skin
under my heat.
"It could be love," you said.

You hate me now,
blue eyes.
You used the
bruises of your old
lovers to build back
something more

and I let the
past leave me
with less.
I could see
no dark spots
in you
but my pain
needed company,
and when once
you thought
love could conquer,
by our epitaph
your eyes
held the ruin of
an idea
abandoned.
"It could've been love," you said.

Who are we now,
blue eyes?
I've erased
the words and the doubt.
I only remember
how your cat ran away
every time I opened the door
and even though
your dad was
a cop I tried
to like him anyway.
We had no vices then.
We could go
to the zoo sober
and smile at turtles

and pet the zebras.
That last time we
drove all night
I reminded you of
those turtles
who seemed to smile back
and we rolled
and kissed
and ignored our sins
and once again
we talked about
forever.
I always try and
go back to
that night I let you
get on the plane
and you left me
and New Jersey behind.
"It can still be love," I said.

I always try and go back to that night.
In my mind.
In my songs.
Because it
was something like love.
We
were something like love.

My Suitcase Is Packed

I know you're home somewhere out there
in Colorado
where the desert flowers
wait all year to turn yellow
and horses with Spanish blood
whip their manes under lightning
as the snows melt down to refill
dried beds.
Somewhere where enough was enough
and you had to put a continent between me
and New Jersey.
I've seen that land and pulled over
to swim naked
where the white crests shatter
and freedom is something more
than a dream.
There are no dead ends on your streets,
the rain only falls straight down
and even stray cats
come when they're called.
I bled for you once
when the war was still far from over
and the end hasn't gotten any closer
so I guess
I'd do it again.

From My Window

The bad reviews came in dozens this time.
I stacked them around my altar
two high
and looked out my window at
the George Washington Bridge.
Would they call me too white
if I did a cannonball
off the upper level?
Do they know what it's like
to write a novel?
Have they ever sat
with their notebooks while
words fell onto the page
like spears from the heavens?
What neighborhood can you live in
when you need time to type a masterpiece?
The bosses want you there at 7 a.m.
Rain. Shine.
Immaculate conception.
Do nothing and have it appear.
Major in education
take the civil servant test.
Time runs out
time runs away
time
time.

It gets to be too much.
Did the poet's parents tell him to get a degree
before moving to The Village?
Did they buy art from the store and leave

plastic stretched around the frame?
How do they know I'm not Bob Dylan?

The fallback plan eclipses the dream.
Die broke with
a blank passport and no epitaph.
Give them what they want.

I watch the intersection under my window
and I think
this could be so easy.
Go to Maine and buy a copy of Uncle Henry's
at 7-11.
Barter for a rifle.
Polish it on the Greyhound home.
Spend the weekend
setting up a perch in my window
while a new hit song about losing
her virginity sings
to me from the stereo.
Percolate a strong cup of black coffee.
Step out into the morning and fire
a few warning shots in the air
like Davy Crockett
on a deer blind.
Watch their feet run around
the sidewalks like ants
dodging a magnifying glass
until finally the pack separates and
one runs right into the cross hairs.

boom.

There are many ways to be remembered.
Just hit one.

Turnpike Blues

He looked at me
as uninterested
and defeated as a 25 year old
on his way to a shitty job
in a shitty town
could, and asked,
  "Have you ever thought about a necktie?
  I mean … why?"
It was a question someone
who hasn't spent hours
driving alone,
to somewhere they didn't want to go,
would never understand.
  I looked at the landscape of the
New Jersey Turnpike, right at the
starting line of what was sure to be
another dead
and eternal winter, and
the air stunk like a chemically enhanced
napalm fart.
  Then I looked down at my necktie
hoping, somehow, it wouldn't be there.
  It was.
I was a manufactured monkey like everyone else.

I lit a cigarette to dilute
the fart smell.
Ernest and I exchanged a silent nod.
     We worked an
       hour later than was scheduled.

If I Could Go Back I'd Change Everything

It's been a little
while since
I took the
typewriter
out.

I've
moved
on, I guess.

Another girl.
A different time.

Those keys
she cleaned
one by one
they don't
work so well
since I threw
it
out of
my window.
I don't know how
it missed the
taxis and the tourists
but it
didn't even
bounce.
It
just sat

there
staring up at me
until I went
down and picked it up.
It's a hex
on my heart
that chills
like a cat
or a guinea pig,
offering nothing,
but I still try and
feed it my soul
sometimes.
And now most
of the keys
refuse to move
or they
jam.

I know
it's
a broken
machine
but sometimes
on nights
when I'm feeling
brave
I'll try
those keys
again
and when
they cross and catch
I'll arrange the

letters
in different
patterns
hoping
there's a message
there,
a riddle
that will lead me
back to her.

You can see
why typewriters
fall like
anvils
from my window.

2:00 a.m. or dawn

You look over at her sleeping sometimes
and wonder
is this the last one?

Bags still packed
clothes unwashed
mattress still on the floor,
a leftover from the last tenant
who lived with nothing stable.
And when I lay on that mattress
my first nights in New York
I knew in my heart that love was just a relic
from centuries covered by dust,
and there was nothing left of me
to exhume those centuries
or at least find someone
who still believed.

But then you're there.
And you realize you've been there for weeks now.
And you ask yourself when it happened.
Was it the night a bartender recognized you
and put a black marker through the bottom of the tab?
Maybe.
Or the night you choked out a taxi driver
who refused to drive her back to Manhattan?
Where have the years gone?
It was winter I think.
I remember her boot prints in the first snow.
The barista who put a shot in our coffee

for an extra dollar.
The subway kid playing Crocodile Rock on a clarinet.
And how our boss didn't come to work that day
because a snow-plow hit his car
so none of us did anything
and I forgot for a while that people are inherently bad.

You look over at her sleeping sometimes
and you know
you've gotten old.
You don't talk to the bartenders anymore.
You don't go anywhere with a line.
You don't feel so bad about kids in cages.
You look back and realize you made all the wrong friends.
Dated all the wrong girls.
Said I love you to all the wrong people.
And it makes you exhausted
but it never makes you fall asleep.

You think about all the hearts you've been handed
and how they all came with a curse.
Except this one.
This one is still easy.
We are not the same but we are simple.
Like the amen after an arduous homily,
you can bow your head and be thankful.
For the first time
asking nothing from anyone.
For the first time
happy you're here instead of anywhere else.
And if you're afraid nothing will ever be new again
just remember the last time you were free
and how you spent it all praying to be found.

Time Won't Save Us Now

I sit above
them at my
desk and look
down at the bars.

All the bars,
all with
400 IPA's on tap
and 80 imported bottles.
And they come
from parts of the
world I used
to dream about going
but it seems
impossible
now that a place like
Prague actually
exists
and you can go there if you want
and the people there
are sitting
and drinking
just like you.

And when I think about Prague
I feel like they
just *know*
and they never
feel the tension.

They can
sit and drink
and waste time
because
they can't fall far enough
to bypass pity.
They'll never know
American blame.

And they scream
downstairs
and fight
and the girls cry
into cell phones
at men with
good haircuts
and boating shoes
and tucked-in polo shirts.
They rule my city now.
And they follow the
girls and
promise them something
I can't.

In
New York
it doesn't matter
if you
can dress yourself.
A good haircut here
costs $150
a week.
In a city

where no one drives
that says
the same
thing
about a man
a Maserati does
somewhere else.

And
it still
says
the same
thing
about me.

2nd grade.

The carnival rolled through town
and he saw the gorilla
with a chain around its neck
and the clowns that got no laughs
and it was his father's weekend to have him
so he got extra popcorn
and the $5 voucher
to ride the donkey around the stable.

His father stole him that night
and he watched the exit home
pass by his window
but he didn't say, "Take me back".
We'd read about Lake Erie
that week in school
and he dreamed of eating
hot dogs in Cleveland
with sour cream instead of ketchup
and getting so full
that when he lay on his back
seagulls would land on his stomach
and what a great picture that would make.

But the car didn't drive west.
They refueled in Suffern
and stayed at a Knights Inn
behind downtown Syracuse.
His father only had enough for one bed
so he gave his son a pillow

and a towel
and made him sleep next to the radiator.
It leaked all night
and the next morning
when they tried crossing into Canada
he watched the police point guns
at his father's head
and drag him out of the car.

The whole thing happened
in about forty-two hours
but it had already made the newspaper
and everyone in town was whispering
that they'd both been murdered.
He was back in class by Tuesday
and told us that upstate
they advertised naked girls on bright billboards
and he was pretty sure
he'd heard someone say
there was no such thing as Santa Clause
and we all nodded as we realized
it was over.

That first letdown felt like the bottom.
We didn't know there would be many more.
And they would all be caused by people
we said we loved.
And they would all be worse.

Sit With Me

Can you sit with me please?
I'm ready to tell those
stories you should've heard
before
I made you
unforgiving.
I've written them to you now,
in each letter -
pulled out
put down.
You know
the ones? Two stamps
in case my feelings become too
heavy.
Another weight
I don't mean to make you carry.
Can you sit with me please?
I can put us onto paper
now, more than this
loneliness
more than this regret.
I can lock us in love
I can lock us in time.
We can be in old books on a shelf,
Used and traded and passed
back and forth,
and put a smile
on the face of all those
who come after us.

What if we could make their world better?
I can't do it without you
I can't.

We're Half Way There

They promised me it was over
but it never ended
it just got worse.
And the shifts grew longer
and the aliens flew away
and the U-Boats swam home
and nothing good ever happened.
The chickens got fat
and America dropped the blinds on the nightmare
plaguing everyone
who never made it off the sacred rock.
The one all great-greats sailed here from
when the sun still set
on another empire.
And the lucky ones learned
you don't look back
when it's all on the line,
you buy a Happy Meal
and drive to death
in a 99' Toyota Camry
while singing the chorus of
"Livin' On A Prayer."

I Wish This Didn't Happen

Remember when you got the guts
to tell me
I'd never be happy?
While you were crying
and naked
waiting for me to understand
what you already knew?
It was the moment
I realized
I'd always be alone.
I said you were crazy
but a better man
would have called it
bravery.
I can remember your diary
on the floor
lying like a bone,
the inside of you
showing itself to me.
You weren't an artist but
I'll bet a younger you
wanted to be.
And I remember I
only had a hoodie for
the walk home.
The smoke trailed out of
my mouth
from your front door to
my back porch.

The time after that
when you took me back
you asked me,
"Why can't this
just be easy?"

I wanted you to understand
it was never meant to be
that way.
We were just actors
playing characters
on a cold stage.
No notes
or method
or clear understanding
of why the curtain
always falls
exactly
the same way.

We were born under the same moon.
Shared the same bad sign.
And it worked for awhile
because you saw life
for what it could be
and I saw life
for what it was.
But there's no peace
for people like me.
All those hours you spent
smiling in your sleep
I knew *they* were closing in.
So I never slept.

And I wondered about
my home in the sky
or my hole
in the ground.

I hope you know
what I know now.
That *they* were closing in for you.
But it wasn't
to take you.
They built a wall around you
that showed itself sometimes.
When light fought its way
through leaves and
windows
and under doors
like carpets
to warm your feet.
It was never easy
because I never
had faith in anything.
I was just like the rest of them.
And I loved you
because
you weren't
like any of them.

I forgot about all that.
And light was always around,
I just never noticed
until it stopped
shining on us.

Everyone Hates You

Everyone hates you.
Even if you haven't figured it out yet
dont worry
you will.
It'll be the confirmation of your biggest fears.
Your father saw something better.
Your readers thought there
was promise.
But they were wrong.
Anyone who has ever believed in anything is wrong.
Even after you put your grandfather in the ground,
after the speech about how you used to sail around
the swamps of eastern Maryland
and put chicken in crab traps
to see what kinds of turtles swam in for the flesh,
you'll be wrong.
About how he was your hero once.
You were wrong.
And then your aunt will find his diary.
And you'll read that he was like everyone else.
That he thought you were born with all the promise
and yet you wasted it
on a stupid major
on the women you followed like a new gospel
and all the forgotten words in your notebook
that never amounted to a decent novel,
that you would fall further
than your privilege should've allowed.
And you'll think about your appetite

and how it far exceeds your talent.
And you won't fight back
because you'll know
he was right.

Buying Cocaine For R*** M******

I was just about to quit for good.
It was another day carrying bags
up and down stairs
while guests stood
in front of the elevators
and complained that they
were taking too long.
Guests who had just gotten done
bitching about the lobby,
that the air conditioning
was "too cold",
that New York had
"too many rats".

Usually I skipped the elevators
and hoofed it up the stairs
with their luggage strapped
to each shoulder.
It gave me five minutes without them.
And if they'd already pissed me off
I might accidentally
drop their bags a few times.

I wouldn't even wait for them
at their rooms.
It was the same story every day.
They had no cash
or they only had euros
or they would pretend

to forget my tip altogether.
But that night I didn't
punish the bags,
I just left them on the floor
and decided
I'd rather be homeless.

There were always windows
you could open
and step out onto fire escapes
for a quick leap,
or empty rooms
with fresh sheets and
high rafters.
But that night was the first time
I realized you could just walk out.
It wasn't against the law yet.

I thought about it on the way
down the stairs,
and I probably would've done it
but then I saw *her* in the lobby -
a famous actress I'd had a crush on
since the days
we bought tickets for
singing animal movies
and then slipped into
the R rated theater
when no one was looking.

I grabbed her bags but I didn't
take the stairs,
I stood right next to her

the whole way.
"How's your day going?"
she asked.
"Terrible," I said. "I was just about to quit
and then you walked in."
She smiled.
I had said the right thing.
I couldn't believe it.
I looked back at my coworkers.
They couldn't believe it.

When we got to her room
I asked her if she'd ever been
to New York before.
Of course she'd been to New York.
Hell, she was the girl I thought of
when I thought of New York.
But she laughed.
Everything that came out
of my mouth was stupid,
but it was coming out right.
"What else do you do?" she asked.
I told her I was a writer.
"What are you working on?"
"I just had a book published," I said. "Would
you read it?"
"A real book?" she asked. "Sure."

I kept about 30 copies of my book
in a locker
downstairs for just this reason.
I went to get one
and there was some crisis

in the lobby.
My manager asked me for help
but I shook my head.
There was more at stake
than keeping my job.

When I handed my book to her I said,
"They're poems, but they don't, like, rhyme."
She gave me a $10 tip
(the most I'd ever been paid for my writing)
and I left,
wondering about this world I had entered,
always surrounded by
fame and money
and none of it ever crossing over.

We never had a lunch break
at that hotel,
you just left
whenever you wanted
and when you got bored
you went back.
This was down on Ludlow Street
so I walked to the Cake Shop
and ordered a Budweiser.
It was happy hour and the bartender
slid two in front of me.

I was pretty drunk after
an hour of that.

My phone was buzzing the entire time
but I ignored it.

When I got back the girl
at the front desk jumped up.
"Where have you been?"
"Working," I frowned.
"*She* called down!" the girl said. "*She* wants you
up in her room."

I rode the elevator looking at myself
in the reflection
of the brass doors.
This was my moment.
She's read my book, I thought.
*She's going to take me away from
all of this.*

Her door was open when I got there.
A guy was sitting on the floor
strumming a guitar.
He wasn't good.
She introduced us and I could tell
by his indifference he was some
LA kid,
born rich,
and all he had to do
was be at that right club
on the right night
and now she was his.

"You're a great writer," she said. "That's why
I need your help."
I was a bellman,
I would get fired
if I didn't do what she wanted,

and usually, this meant
I would get arrested
if I got caught.
"I need to finish a script,"
she said. "Can you get me a bag?"
I swore I'd never do it again,
but what the hell?
"How much
do you want?" I asked.
The guy with the guitar was
finally interested.
"Get two," he said.

She handed me $300.

It was a new hotel and
I'd never bought coke
in that neighborhood before.
Janis was my favorite cocktail waitress
and she was running
the lobby bar by herself.
But Janis was a soldier.
I told her what I needed
and she left her customers and
took me to another bar.
"I know a guy
with the best coke," she said.

I looked at her nose.
I watched her inhale a cigarette.
Janis had a beauty that ran so deep
all her hard work
couldn't betray it.

She took me to Max Fish and
her guy charged $100 a gram.
That was a crazy price
and the bag looked really light
but Janis had done me a solid
so I gave her $50
as a thank you.

When I got back into the lobby
Ben stopped me.
"We've got to try it out,"
he said. "You can't give
her a bag of shitty blow."
We went up to the manager's office
and did a bump.
Then another.
"Never forget," Ben said, "they're paying us
to snort this right now."

I went up to her room and
she opened the door, drunk.
"Do you have a dog?" she asked.
I knew she was one of the
adopt or die types
so I said "Yeah" but
I didn't elaborate.
She told me a whole story
about white people
and how they're the first
ones to get rid of their dogs
when times get tough.
"I hate everyone," I said. "People
don't deserve dogs."

She liked that.
She took the coke and kissed me
on the cheek.

The next day she told me
she was getting an apartment
around the corner.
It sounded like an invitation.
"I'm leaving New York," I said. "Why do you
only get the girl
after you buy the plane ticket?"
The LA guy parked a convertible
against the curb.
"That's too bad," she said. "It
could've been fun."
Then she walked past me
and threw her suitcase
into the backseat.
She blew me a kiss as she sat
in the passenger side
and put her feet up on the dashboard.
"It could've been fun," she yelled.

The staff looked at me,
waiting for an explanation,
so I gave it to them.
"All the poems in the world won't buy you
a convertible," I said. "I don't know
how many times
I have to learn that lesson
before I stop
trying."

The Woolly Mammoth

Remember back when you were young?
You thought you'd get a diploma
the old-fashioned way.
The first voice of a new generation
screaming, "Get me out of here"
or, "I want to go home."
I heard it down hallways
before we rolled dice
on the bathroom floor.
I heard it like a slave hears
new religion raining from the trees.
From homeroom to the Principal's office,
they tried to take it out, arrest your rage,
but it stunk up every vein in your body
like a clogged sewer,
and you were never afraid to lose it.
"In the womb," you told me once,
"I was unhappy even then."

And then there were the streets.
The bus station in Newark
and the park two blocks down
where the runaways raid
the pigeon coops and
they find dead bums
and cigarette butts dragged out.
It was like a vacation home right on a river,
under buildings like dead peaks so the sun
never shined into your eyes.

It was so you,
every move planned for the great story.
Those were the days you were always
looking forward to.
The envy of every fool.
You wrote your own legend
and it kept me amused.
I used to think that was pretty cool
but I'm invisible now,
I'll fade away
like the woolly mammoth
but you …
you'll live on forever as
some kind of Cinderella,
or a pin-up girl.

Out At Sea

I stand in Easton Maryland now.
She, in Kalispell Montana.
Like two sailors from a ship
that mutinied in different ports
there is a hatred between
what I did and what I'm owed
and what she gave and
what I'd promised.

I remember five years or ten lives ago
watching her on that ship
scanning the horizon.
Sea spray blowing over the deck
like little birds
lost on migration.
Standing at the bow with one hand
on her hip
and the other
in loose salute.
Back straight as a mother
with a pail on her head
walking to thirsty children.

The dawn rose early
and cut the spray down to salt.
I spoke about heading west
or south or north
to any horizon without a town
that really knew us.

But mirrors never scared her
like they did me.
She'd read a story about
eternal return in her youth,
no consequences
plagued her dreams.

We looked off the stern
at dolphins jumping the
highway lines in our wake.
They waved at us
and opened their mouths
and one even had
the same scar on its cheek
my grandpa had come home
from Normandy with.

But I didn't smile back
at those dolphins like she did.
I was too busy praying for the boat
to hit a rock and capsize
far offshore.
I knew there was no dock
in my future without a black flag
and old scraps
even seagulls
wouldn't touch.
And even if I drowned
it still would've been better than
going back
to New Jersey.
And maybe my death
could've finally filled the emptiness
between us.

The Good Fortune Execution

Sometimes I think we are like flowers
so fragile
reaching up from a hard cracked ground
shivering shoulder
to shoulder
waiting to be ripped apart
in the endless storm
like old dirt praying for rain
begging for just a drop
show us *something* is up there
and that *something* cares.

They fill the headlines with
the ones who need
God the most,
lined up against the wall,
blindfolded.
Some get it quick
some get lucky.
The good fortune execution.
No dirt
no planes overhead while the kids
shake back and forth,
hands around their own throats
praying to die.
What a silly God.
He always enjoyed a good show.
And the real headline grabbers
don't end in a sentence,

those kids choke to death in real time.
But God doesn't read the newspaper,
or maybe he does and he just hates the
poor and the weak
the same as everyone else,
only maybe
a little bit more.

Because he does smile on some.
And the chosen ones
thank him
in their speeches and
over their steak dinners.
Wouldn't you?
This world was only made for the rich,
and just because they don't show it
doesn't mean they don't know it.

But the poor have to live here, too.
And while we watch hope fade
like a plane
headed for the horizon
sometimes it's hard to remember that, yes,
we have to live in this country
but we don't have to love it.
And like every other boss I've served under,
God would do a lot better with a
bullet in his head.
And those under him,
crawling on all fours in his shadow,
saying
"Yes sir", "No sir",
saying "Yes please", and "Thank you",

should share a similar fate.
Or maybe something worse.
No blindfold
no execution.
Just the curse
of spending eternity
in his company.

Believe It

There's a mirror on her dresser
with old Polaroid's wedged in the sides
from a time when love was new
and we thought the 60's could come back
and the fuzz from the camera's old filter
looked like something holy
surrounded our world.

She curls her straight hair
in the glass and it holds
while she puts on a new dress
and even though it's New York in August
she can always find a tree in Harlem
standing over the last breezy corner.

She doesn't believe in fairy tales.
I never did either.
But here we are
at Central Park and it's midnight.
And once again there's a girl
I find myself planning a future with
telling me what can never be.

It's always like this.
And tomorrow will always be like that.
Confused. Hungover. Broke.
Checking my wallet to see
if I still have a Metrocard.
And always surprised

that I slept so well
while the pigeons meditated on wires
and she called out of work.

Casino de Montreal

Cashed out
in the backseat
with $2 in quarters
for a slot machine
at the Montreal casino.
Just past the freezing line
and the last American gas station
where latchkey kids
raid dumpsters for old porn
long before their parents
stop buying them pizza
for finishing a novel.

I won $100 on the first pull
and went outside to call my mom
and tell her
I had just failed out of school.
A black guy followed me
and asked for a cigarette
and when I said no
he put a knife to my throat.
I held my hands up
and faster than I had pulled the lever
he emptied my pockets.

I slept facedown on the carpet
of a Chinatown motel for two days
but eventually
I had to eat.

I called my mom and told her
I was broke again,
only this time
it was on a snowbound highway
with no continental breakfast
just outside of Montreal.
I thought it was the good kind of failure
but she didn't agree.

It's hard to be man alive,
full of everything but food,
expecting nothing
but sympathy.

The Heart Of America

I lost another one who didn't want love
or forever
or some way back to
the heart of America.
She just wanted kids.
White kids
named John and Jesse and little Sally.
Kids that would get her off work
and never make her think
about California
and giraffes
or the way she felt at 16
when her parents stopped loving her
but said the words anyway,
who looked at their little girl
and decided she didn't have *it*
so they went to the next one.

She wanted kids who'd adopt a dog
named Lady or Molly,
and a vet who might say "it's 1/4 Pit Bull
but the dog will never stop looking like a Lab."
And the house could be new.
And the kids would never have
their own minds.
They would be patriots
and they would never fail like citizens.
Their mother could change the truth
and never have to explain

that she'd found love once
and it didn't act
like it was supposed to,
that she didn't say, "Hit me"
while age and time were still on her side.
The kids would never want to know
about the heart of America
and that it disappeared
just around the time that
they made it cool
to sell love
for money.

A Pretty Plague

This couch again.
Waking up dry under plants surrendered.
A little thirsty still from
my walk home last night.
The long shift ahead of me but this time
it isn't so bad.
The sous-chef at Dirty French
sees me stealing oysters
and shows me how to slide a knife in
and open
an oyster clean.
A warm night down Ludlow Street
but the sky is winter clear
and I can make out a single star
while I hike across two Villages
and Father Demo Square.

All the old jesters are out holding court,
clutching onto their corners
before Bank Of America and
Dunkin' Donuts put them
on one-way buses
with no stops before
Albany or Troy.
The rat king outside of Katz's
sits still in his wheelchair
waiting for scraps of pastrami.
Punjabi drivers plan sit-ins
and suicides

at the basement deli on Houston.
The last bar light on the Bowery
flickers out like a blinking ghost
and I'm thinking,
"Where am I?
What was the point of this thing
that they sailed oceans for?"

Won't you meet me at Fanelli's?
I want to hear your cello grind
in the libra wind
before
the final last call.
And Bob at the bar, the Serbian prince,
he hates you.
He hates me too.
He loved this city when no fire trucks
came to the rescue.
But we came.
We saved the neighborhood
we can't afford to drink in.
You're about to make it special, though.
Your guy's coming and you've got a coupon.
The bags are $50 and the stuff
is all right.

Cutting lines in the Fanelli's bathroom
on a urinal three hundred years old.
Should we stop and
appreciate the history here?
What did George Washington do
on this porcelain?
A fork in the road for all of history.

He went left
and saved the world.
I went the other way and
woke up with you
on that shitty Williamsburg sand,
covered in slime with
a cold wind against our ears.
And if I could go back
I wouldn't change a thing.
Because this world
always deserves a good story.
And so many have fought in revolutions
but so few
have fallen in love.
And while I watched your lips
back away
from your teeth so a smile
could paint your face
I knew that nothing
they ever fought for
could mean more than that morning.

The Twilight's Last Gleaming

It's not funny
I'm not hungry
I wish I died before the 90's came back
but no one retires at the right time.
The fade is a slow burn
and usually the ones who
could've been good
drop out first.
They name baseball fields after them
probably a scholarship
but no one alive cares,
memories replaced too soon
by the next draft.
And no ghosts hang like frames
in these halls,
the dead don't want any part of this shit
either.

No one is well.
The fast clap of the audience was
muted long ago.
The people needed to eat and
stole the generator.
The NYPD shot at the black ones
and the white working class
didn't like it this time.

No one is well.

They turn the lights on
but the audience doesn't laugh.
The twilight last gleamed on
some other era when we
didn't have to hide
from the dawn
and everyone could still smile
at the mirror.

To The Girl I Went On A Date With Last Night

Your songs
never got sadder,
how can that
be?
Your mother
still
has your father,
you held onto
your God,
I didn't
know
the world
still deserved
something like
that.

Yeah
I'll go to Brooklyn.
I'll pay for the booze.
I'll walk you around.
We can stand
and watch
the sun go down
behind
the last projects of lower Manhattan.
I'll wonder if I invented you.
And I'll wonder if you'll erase me.
I've got the torch in

my hand.
Don't turn
your face too quickly,
even a breeze
will give the flames
a reason
to dance.

You've got
the after storm blue eyes.
Your eyes
tell me you've sat on this bench before.
You
know
which two buildings
the sun
will split. It's
the knowledge
of a broken heart.
Even with your God
and
your parents
love has been a betrayal.
You spent too much
time on this bench
alone. You
know
the bums,
you know which hipster
will bring the guitar
and what song he
will sing.
You can't know these things

until you're alone. And
you can't
be alone
until you've
learned
you're only safe
with
yourself.

It's hard
to know when
to make a move.
The last light has
attached itself
around your
head
like an
icon,
the divine glow,
whatever
that yellow
ring
is circling the white dove
that means
peace and love
and the sun
and spring
and youth.
I know I should
kiss you now
but I don't
because
you say,

"Let's swim to
Manhattan"
and
in the water's reflection
I realize I'd rather see you smile
than see
your face touching mine.

And maybe
it
should end like that.
With us
not touching.
And I could know
you
like the
birds know the sky.
And I won't have to invent you.
And you'll never have to erase me.
Your songs
will stay sweet
and we
can share the dark places
of our hearts
that
no one else
gets to see.
I'll
love you
like only a man
who never gets the girl
can,
and every day

will feel like
those
last minutes
we put our heads
to the ground,
figuring out
how to
share our first kiss
goodbye.

The Oath

We slit our wrists to the side
and put them together
and you told me your father
had been murdered
as our lines crossed and nothing
internal knew no boundaries.
We didn't die like I thought we would
and you spread our blood around your face
like war paint,
two checks under your brown eyes.
I tuned my guitar and you danced naked
like a shaman
while I strummed an old folk song.
My parents were looking for a second house
in Florida
and I forgot to feed my mom's fish
and the dogs thought we were insane
but we were happy.
And in the kitchen
we laid down
like we owned the floor.
And we bled together on my mom's new tile
like love
burrowing into the earth.

When I see a pair of ducks
flying together to the ends of the map
I think of you, the one who gave me
more than her heart,

the one who
opened herself up.
And even though we didn't make it
to the end of the earth
I slept well and
I woke up in a better world.

My First Night Back

We were far apart once
but you can hear my heart now
in this chest.
And your hair used to itch
my skin if you didn't tuck it back
but you'll never hear about it again
because I left you once
and I learned
to miss everything -
coffee at sunset
and all-night sirens up and down
Amsterdam
while the pit bulls howled at
newspapers blowing by like
white rabbits taunting them
in the night.
And the coffee fades while the rum kicks in
and all those sounds fade to the periphery
like a television in someone
else's apartment.
And your hair crawls across my chest
like the tiny arms of a friendly spider.
You always knew what you had
but it took me a little longer.
There's no escape in my forever now,
our bones can grow soft in peace.
And that future we always talked about
can't come soon enough.

Can We Live Like This?

It didn't take so long
did it?
Your story's
in your
smile, those lips
once said,
"I'll
never
love again."

I know
you're a fighter, kid.
Life
didn't take
it's time
with
you. But you're
not so bored,
there's still a light
in there.
Sure,
you
can sway
like the
breezy
palm trees
of your hometown,
but I don't
want to

know
if you can bend ...
can you break?

I remember
your greasy
hair from
the plane,
your legs crossed
on the white sheets,
the slow surrender
of your eyes
when you realized
I thought
you
were beautiful.
It was sudden
and eternal.
I chose you
to erase
all my sorrows.
Will you?
You see
life in the raw
and that makes me
trust you.
We know
when
we
find
our own.

I think
about what it
will be like.
The coffee.
The date.
The booze.
The bed.
The cigarette.
But
I can
leave those
for the men
that came
before.
I
want
your window,
to
watch
the breeze
through the leaves
of those palms
and wonder
if this life
actually
existed before
you got here.

The Last Streetlight In Heaven

Heaven's filling up with diplomas
from a youth
waiting single file
on the will call line.
And they listen to the crows
circling overhead
who learned a verse back when
they nested above the schools.
"It doesn't look like Verona
anymore," they say.
"There's a dirt pit
where the swimming pool was."

I hope the boys can use
their track marks
as road maps
and hold the hands of girls
who sold their final sacraments
on the Newark streets.
Where spring feels like December,
where glass clogs the gutter,
and no price is too high
for a whole generation to erase
some of its hunger.

These towns flood now
but the rains never come.
There are enough mothers' tears
to water the lawns.

And in every man's poverty
we can see
the origin of night.
The first syringe.
The absence of God.
We were a class once but nothing is left.
And there's no sky clear enough
for the lucky ones to
reckon under.

A whole history of past sins
built above
Indian bones.
The interest keeps rising on
America's crimes.
Our parents lined up to vote
and prayed
it would always stay the same,
but the hurricane comes
and the shattered glass
gets washed away,
and they keep signing up fresh faces
to take its place.

Lorraine

I didn't know she was drunk
until
she threw up across her desk.
They say, "Don't write about love
because it's lame
because it's all been said before
because by now
  everyone knows it doesn't exist."

But this was it.
The real thing.
All the burning
and desires
  the smell of Rhone
  the smell of rain
she wretched back and forth and
the fish tank lights of fluorescent classrooms
found their subject.

The rest of the class sat in front of their computers
like rookies in a police academy.
Obedient
loyal
sipping cups of coffee for a clarity that wouldn't come,
becoming machines in hopes of not being replaced by them.
  Like the scabs who cross picket lines
  like the prisoner of war who builds bullets
getting a paycheck today to extinct tomorrow.

But not her.
She is a rebel
in a time
where cool has died
and the new revolution
won't be televised
or free wi-fied.

And in an age where being dangerous
is going vegan
and recycling plastic straws,
sometimes
all it takes is public vomiting
to prove
that you are still free.

My Bluest Valentine

Don't bake me a birthday cake
this year.
Let's go to Wawa and
buy a carton
of our old cigarettes
and drive to the Poconos,
to the mini golf
where we made dirty bets
around the windmill
and both of us got a rash
that night from the
heart-shaped hot tub.
Or we can go back
to your parents' basement
with the wood paneled walls
and the one cold night
we slept under the heater
and you whispered,
"Pretend it's Aspen."
Let's get married this time
like we swore we would at seventeen
when all we wanted
was to do drugs and fall in love
and we were still young enough
to be good at both

Fish Tank

I believed in everything
when I was twenty
except when you told me
your tree had been cursed.
The Dow Jones crashed that day
or maybe
it was before the end of all things,
back when we watched Saddam's body double
drop through the floor
and the crowd cheered
as the noose tightened.
We didn't look away from the computer screen
and I don't think I did again
until your mom showed up and
dumped my fish tank
full of fancy guppies down the toilet.
You packed your YSL heels back in the box
while I yelled at your mom
and no one listened
as I explained how hard it had been
to get those fish to breed.
No one listened at the bar that night either.
And I guess you were right,
love's only a cure until it becomes a regret.
But you could've just left a note when you
decided to break my heart.
I don't know why the fish had to die too.

Driving To Thom Young's House

I heard there were no gun laws in Texas
so I rented a Taurus and drove
to Thom Young's house,
running over prairie dogs and singing the new
Blake Shelton Christmas song.
And when I got there
I bought a rifle and some nightcrawlers
and we fished in a puddle behind the Allsup's.
But the fish didn't want any worms
and on the drive back
Thom said Led Zeppelin wouldn't make it today.
And I remembered the music
and how it had lived in me once
and in my dreams
I can still hear my mother sing it like
she's hanging over my crib.
And sometimes the college radio
comes in clear from Amarillo
and Thom finds an old box of tobacco
and we smoke like kings without a throne,
flicking ash at the coyotes circling the porch.
Once upon a time betting on
whether it would be them
or us
but we don't play that game as much anymore.
And on cold Sunday's after Christmas
we leave burritos outside for the dogs

The Santa Fe Trail

You can read maps by starlight
in places I've been
and you sleep like shit off the Mexican beer
and wake up covered in bites
in hotels where life is impossible
and anything still breathing
wants blood.
Did you know what you wanted
at the taco truck in Dalhart?
Do you know that there's a
whole country out there
that doesn't care about New York?
I do now.
I might know everything now.
I've drank from the shallow creeks.
I've chewed the taco rellenos with
fire still in the seeds.
I looked up for God and every grackle
in the tree followed my gaze.
Next time I'll follow the trails in the sand
and the small streams will lead me to the
Window Rock.
Or maybe the other way -
to lie down in a graveyard
where desert rats use cow skulls as ashtrays.
And if the rains ever come again
maybe white petals
will bud up from my bones
and a lost rabbit can
spend a day
sleeping under my shade.

Beautiful Things

There are beautiful things tucked into your bed
and late some nights
I would watch you lie there
and smile in your sleep.
A happiness I never knew.
And I thought maybe
if I stayed with you awhile
you could show me how that felt.
I was a wet cigarette,
I was a dog you brought in from the cold,
and I stopped thinking about death so much
once I found something
worth the epilogue.
Writing is never easy
but it stops
when you're in love.
That endlessness
you were always trying to conquer
is suddenly too small.
It's a foreign country
but a language you speak,
and all the words in all the notebooks
read like they were written for one girl.
So keep your eyes closed
and keep smiling
like we're owed this world.
There was a whole universe once
outside your room
but my memory

is gone.
I can't remember anything else
I was ever searching for.

Stony Hill

The neighbors used to call the cops on us
at least
two times a week.
The other five
were the days
that we quit drinking.
I was only happy when I was with her.
We only drank
when we were together.
Sometimes
 I needed to work.
Sometimes
 she needed to paint.

I remember those days
sitting in the back of a white van,
driving from Long Island City to Wall Street,
carrying ladders and curtains
down alleys
to service elevators,
watching for the sun
to do its revolution over the
empire state building,
drowning itself
in the hudson,
finally allowing
me
to drive turnpikes
and parkways

to get home
to her.

She'd wake up at five
or six.
From October to April
I don't think she ever saw
the sun.
We stole cat food so we had money for weed.
We didn't eat because of the cocaine.
  But I kept working
  and she kept sleeping.
My parents wanted to know why
she didn't get a job.
How could I explain the obvious?
She was too beautiful for work
  for orders
 for discipline
and for a girl who knows this
there's no such thing as enough.

My back hurt all the time from the grind.
My face hurt all the time from her fists.

I'll never live with a Puerto Rican again.
When she got bored she left.
When she got angry she hit.
We fought hard.
We made up hard.
  The neighbors called the law for both.
Each would leave me
bleeding
and bruised.

And when the cops showed up
it was hard to explain
 that I was actually having the best time of my life.

Jersey Shore

There you were
on that Jersey sand
in a white bikini
like Marilyn Monroe
pinned up on a teenagers wall
or in a jail cell
over a fresh coat of paint.
A girl from a different era
when everything was good
and no sea turtles
swallowed six-pack rings
and I could take my baby
down the parkway
to the casino lights
on a Saturday night.

You'd heard about me
but we were kings and queens
so I asked you out anyway.
And you looked back at your friends'
shaking heads
and saw that they cared about your sanity
not your happiness
so you said yes.
I knew forever
could start like that
so I made a mixtape for the drive
and picked you up at seven.

You were a dream I'd been saving
since my first life
and your mother
saw it on my face when
she answered the doorbell,
so she sent you out
into a stranger's arms
and didn't worry like she used to.

I remember your high score at the arcade
and the four free pinballs
that dropped in
when you broke the last record.
There wasn't much you were bad at -
at least I can't remember anything now -
and how about that sunrise
over the Asbury waves
when we bummed a cigarette
and squinted our eyes into darkness
while the sun took the night
and gave us back our youth?

You told your friends about
every other night.
I'll bet they never heard of that one.

Just Like W. 3rd At Midnight

I can get through the day
feeling lonely or nothing at all.
But lately
I've been standing on my fire escape -
watching a dog who can't catch its tail -
wondering why
nothing
underneath me
is beautiful anymore.
Where's the small girl with spring freckles
who smiles at funerals?
With eyes like subway lights
that crawl around corners
long before the train arrives?
Don't I have enough left
to lose a little more?

It can be you.
The girl from Oslo or Rome
waking up alone right now.
Is your ashtray still smoking?
Do you have a story you wrote at sixteen
when your notebook
was covered in stars
and all of our parents
were going to stay married?
I'll bet those pages were the same as mine.
Was it hard for you like it was for me
when you lost the handle

but time kept moving?
And do you
feel the same as me
when you look to the west?
Did the boys of your hometown give
you a chance?
Did they ask about your rising sign
or the things your hair does
under the streetlights?
I'm jealous of that first face
and the lips you lost
forever on.
That's the victory for some
but I promise it was never mine.

What if we sailed to the coast
of my ancestors
and let today be just like yesterday?
Would you want to share a lifetime of nothing?
Just a white room
and an old dog
or a beach with no trap doors
where I can be held with no fear
and give you
everything
that still lives in me.

It takes me longer to get
where the rest seem to start
but that's not
your problem.
I've seen your fawned eyes glow
under every moon

so keep your hair long
and I'll push it behind your ears.
And maybe in the morning
I can name your belly button
and we'll smile
like it's the first time
every time.

Just turn the record over before
we say goodnight.
I want to hear you sing some more.

A Place For Everyone

Do you remember the first time?
I went to the place where
all the lost wishes go that lovers
make on stars
but never hit their mark.
A place beyond the sun
that died long before
the first man
loved the first woman.
And if time traveled as fast
as youth
as loss
as regret
we wouldn't have to spend
so much of it looking back.
We could stand on each other
like a pyramid of hearts,
one beating love that
could never break,
or a hive that moves
the stragglers along
so no one is left.
Because the blue we stare at
that turns into black
has been there for years
and switches like the channels
on a television set.
So don't worry,
I won't bury you when you're gone.

I'll climb the mountain and lie down
on the rocks.
I'll stare up at the space beyond the sun,
that place they say no one has been
but we both know they're wrong.
Every smile, every tree
has some remnant of a God.
And we know that place
they come from
belongs to everyone.

The Clock Set Back

The shadows come early as the middle
shifts closer to the sides.
Children cup their hands under the blind bird
and their giggles warm the schoolyard
when she drops a worm for fun.
A wet tickle in their palms as it curves down
and nestles into the ravines of their new veins.

So shallow.
So easy to steady.

Old night-lights ground the runway
when the triangle calls them home.
No desert in their smiles
walking hand in hand
underneath a scarred and coming moon.
Feathers replace the leaves.
Old wars still fought.
They don't know yet that all things
can split or shatter
or fray from the seams.
Even when mothers stop crying,
and everything once declared empty
fills up.

There's another end to all migrations.
Other sidewalks the birds will sing above.
A place water sleeps under bridges and dirt
and cormorants drift with the current

until a fence cuts them off.
The pyramids crumbled to dust
in those backyards
but still
no desolation pales their eyes.
They weren't born from love,
and free of its promise
they can fly from winters
from summers
from shadows and sun.
Even at the mercy of the same moon
they'll never be martyrs
of something unsown.

There's an empty branch out there awaiting
a new breeze.
Just above the dreaming puppies.
Just above the rabbits waiting patiently
for the coming thaw.
Plain as the cormorants coat.
Plain as the worms digging new tunnels.
Plain as the leaves growing brighter dead.

A Garden East Of Eden

If I could do it all over again
there's not much I would do the same.
I would say I love you a lot more
to a lot less people.
I would only find brick walls on black and white streets
to kiss against.
I would buy a shag carpet every day
and lay in it.
And I would never eat until my chest was thin as paper
so you could see that
my heart
looks
like
a heart.

And every time I say
the house will always smell like fresh flowers
I'll mean it
and every car door I can open for you
I'll open it
And every cage that holds a turtle
I'll free it
And every dog that has no home
I'll adopt it
And every door in the house that isn't painted yellow
I'll paint it
and every bike that has a basket
I'll fill it

And if I promise you that I'm over it
I will be.

But if I say
I don't want you to love me any more than you do
I'll still be lying,
and I'll hope that you are still smarter than me,
and you won't change a thing.